RISING STAR

English

Written by **Akanksha Arora**
Edited by **Priyanka Dey**
Illustrated by **Neeraj S. Roy**
Designed by **Nirbhay Kumar**

Acknowledgement: Manmeet Narang

www.pegasusforkids.com

Published by Kuldeep Jain for B. JAIN PUBLISHERS (P) Ltd., D-157, Sector 63, Noida - 201307, U.P

Printed in India

PREFACE

In their pre-primary years children need concrete experiences or connections with real life. If they see a purpose in what they are doing, they develop interest, following which learning is inevitable. The English alphabet is a collection of abstract symbols for children. It is important for them to understand that the letters they recognize and write are a part of their immediate surroundings. Since all books, newspapers, boards, and advertisements use the print form, we are introducing the upper case and lower case letters simultaneously in this book. Children will recognize both, but will write upper case letters only, as simpler strokes are involved in writing them.

The book gives children ample exposure to words. They are not expected to read at the beginning. Pictures given with the words help them make sense of the word and lead to sight learning. Children are not expected to memorize the spellings. Gradually, with exposure, they will learn to read and write the words on their own.

In this book, we have not followed the regular A-Z sequence to introduce letters. Our sequence is such that after learning 3-4 letters, children start reading and making words with those letters. This gives them a sense of accomplishment. However, the same will not be possible if we follow the regular sequence, which leads children to forget the letters covered earlier as they progress to the new ones.

The book includes stories after some letters are covered. These stories use words with only the letters covered till then. Children can start reading with assistance and can gradually read on their own.

CONTENTS

A B C D E F G

H I J K L M N

O P Q R S T U

V W X Y Z

RHYME

A, B, C, D, E, F, G, H, I, J, K,L, M, N, O, P, Q,R, S, T, U, V, W, X, Y, Z

XYZ Sugar on the bread. If you don't like it, better go to bed. Early in the morning, come to me, I will teach you, ABC.

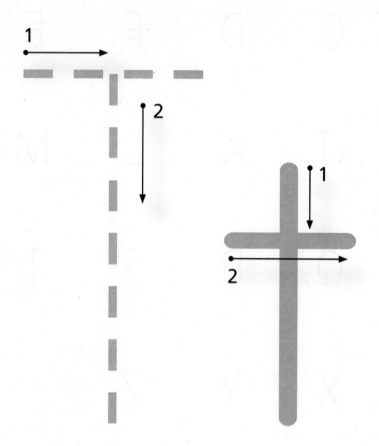

Words that begin with T

Telephone

Table

Tiger

Tongue

Tortoise

Turnip

Tomato

Tyre

Tree

More words with the sound of T

Basket

Water

Bat

Carrot

Parrot

Hat

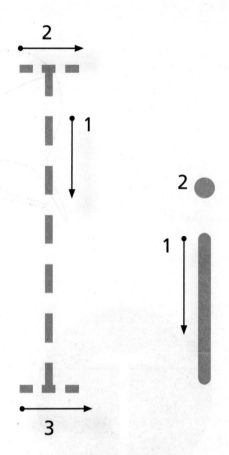

Words that begin with I

Iron

Inkpot

Igloo

Ice

Island

Ice cream

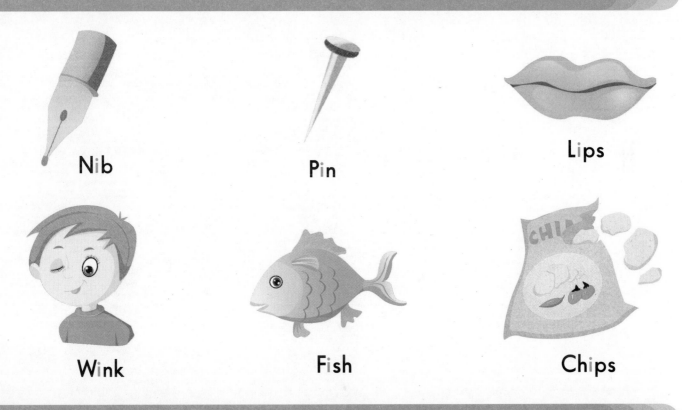

Nib

Pin

Lips

Wink

Fish

Chips

It   Kit   Sit   If

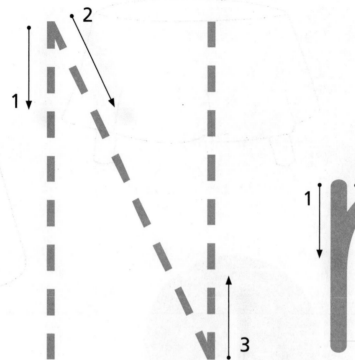

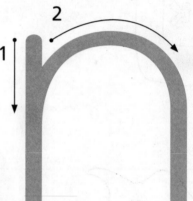

Words that begin with N

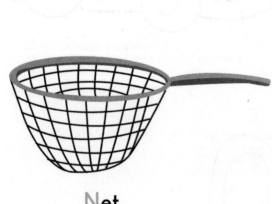

Net

Nib

Nest

Newspaper

Needle

Nail

Neck

Nurse

Ant

Hand

Pants

Sun

Lion

Fan

Let's read

| In | Tin | Sink | Fin |

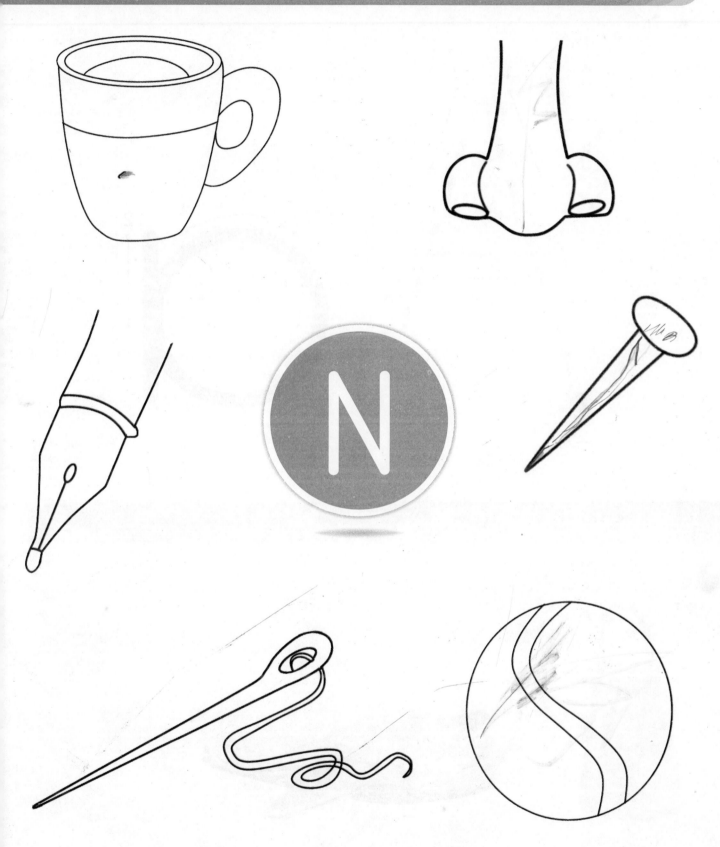

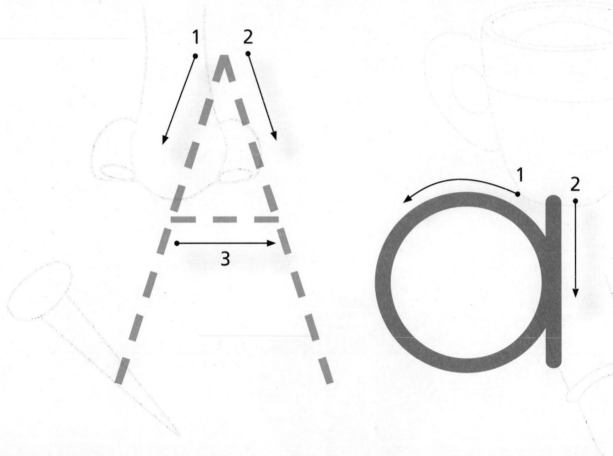

Words that begin with A

Apron   Aircraft   Arm

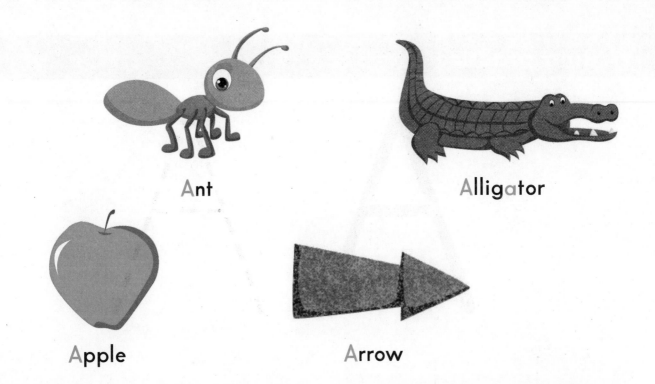

Ant

Alligator

Apple

Arrow

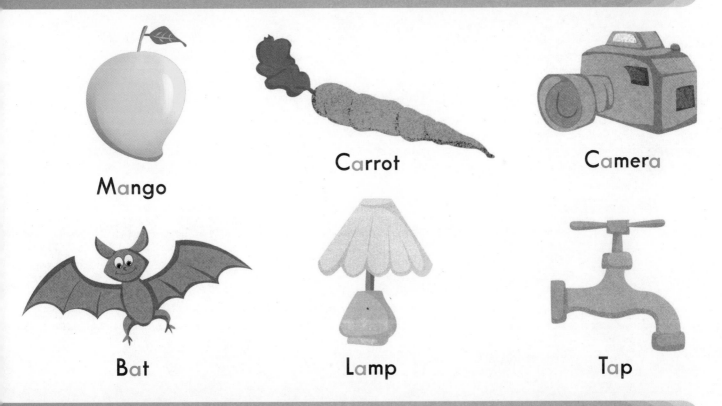

Mango

Carrot

Camera

Bat

Lamp

Tap

Let's read

| An | Ant | Tan |

I Learn, I Remember

In each box, colour the picture whose name begins with the letter shown.

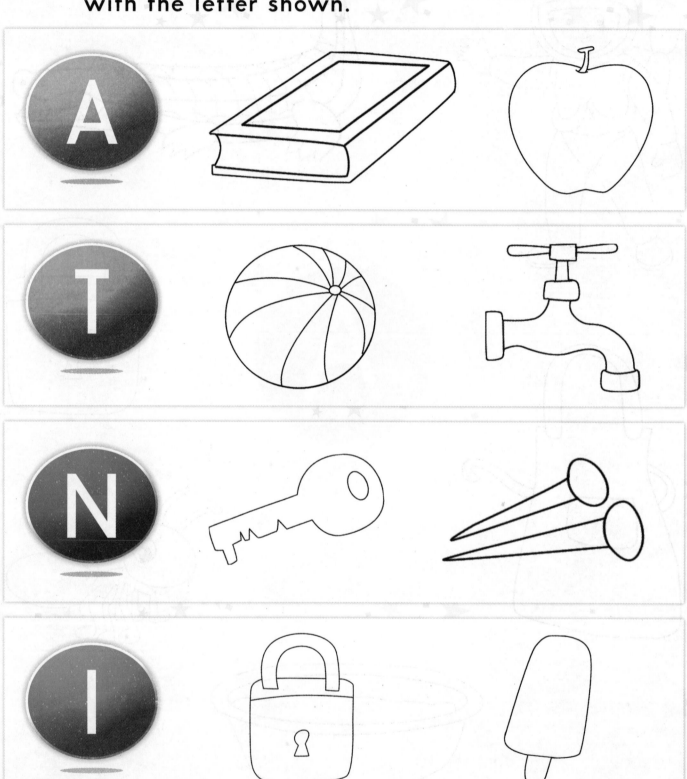

T   I   N   A

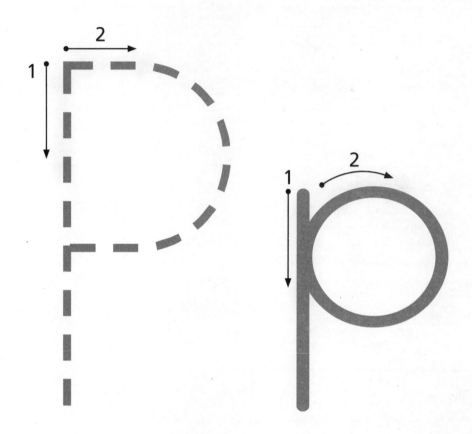

Words that begin with P

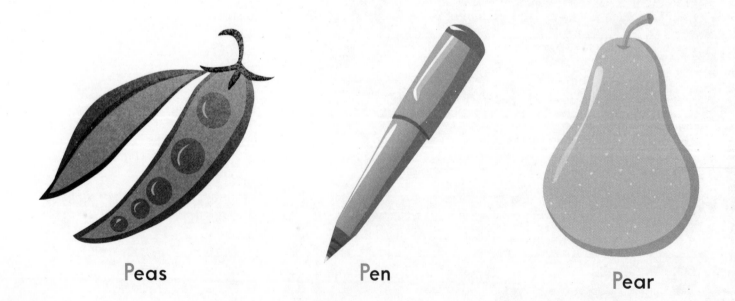

Peas

Pen

Pear

Parrot

Pumpkin

Penguin

Potato

Pencil

Pin

More words with the sound of P

Cap

Apple

Lips

Lamp

Ship

Grapes

Let's read

| Pit | Pan | Pat | Tap | Tip | Nap |

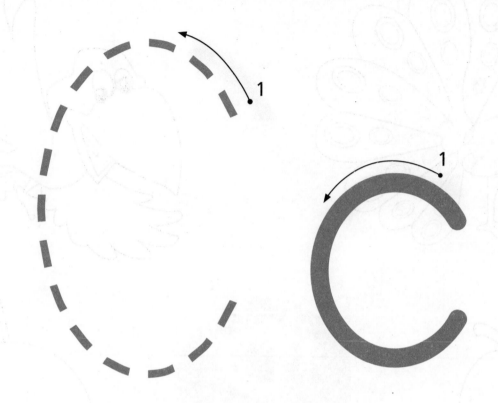

Words that begin with C

Carrot

Cap

Cow

Cat

Cup

Cake

Crow

Carpet

Clock

More words with the sound of C

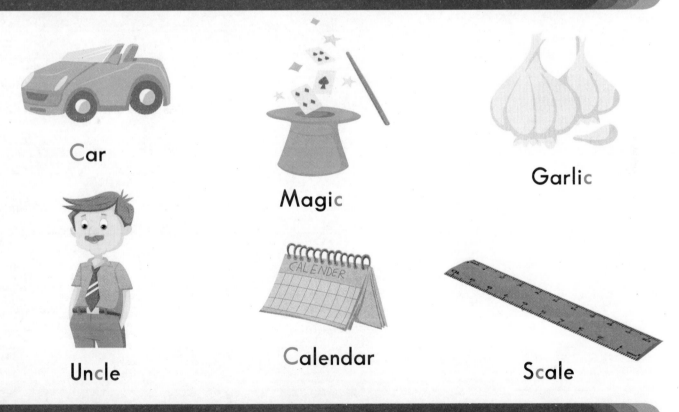

Car

Magic

Garlic

Uncle

Calendar

Scale

Let's read

| Act | Can | Cape | Coat |

Words that begin with S

Sun

Snake

Star

Swan

Sock

Soap

Sofa

Scooter

Spoon

More words with the sound of S

Ba**s**ket

Gla**ss**

Bu**s**

Ca**s**k

Ma**s**k

Skirt

Let's read

| **S**it | **S**ip | Can**s** |

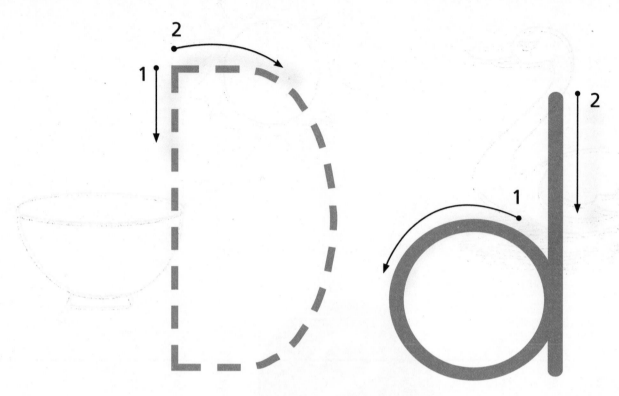

Words that begin with D

Deer · Doll · Donkey

Duck

Dolphin

Doctor

Dustbin

Drum

Door

More words with the sound of D

Win**d**ow

Gar**d**en

Me**d**al

Be**d**

Sli**d**e

Can**d**le

Let's read

| Sad | Pad | Dip | And | Sand |

Picture Reading

1. Who all do you see in the picture?
2. What are they doing?
3. What toys do you see?

Practise writing these letters.

P   C   S   D

I Learn, I Remember

In each box, colour the picture whose name begins with the letter shown.

 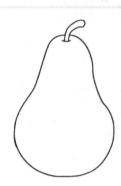 

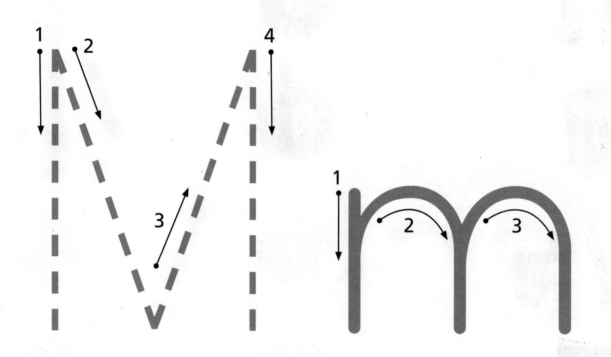

Words that begin with M

Mat

Mango

Mouse

Man

Milk

Mask

Moon

Mug

Melon

More words with the sound of M

Camera

Lemon

Ice cream

Camel

Tomato

Lamp

Let's read

| Map | Dim | Mint | Mist | Camp | Damp |

M M

M M M M M M

M M M M M M

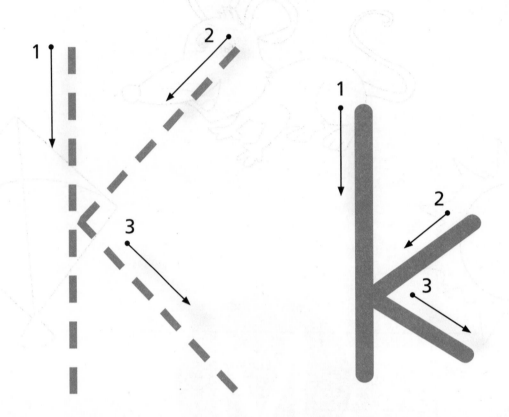

Words that begin with K

Kite

King

Kettle

Kiwi   **Kangaroo**   **Key**

More words with the sound of K

Milk   **Monkey**   **Fork**

Cake   **Lake**   **Book**

Let's read

Kit   Ink   Kind   Skin   Skit   Ask

How to Make H

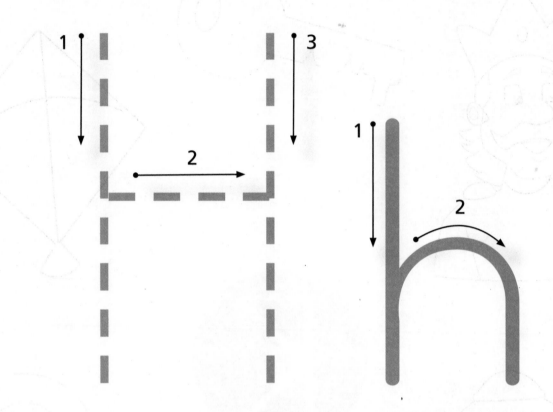

Words that begin with H

Hat

Hen

Horse

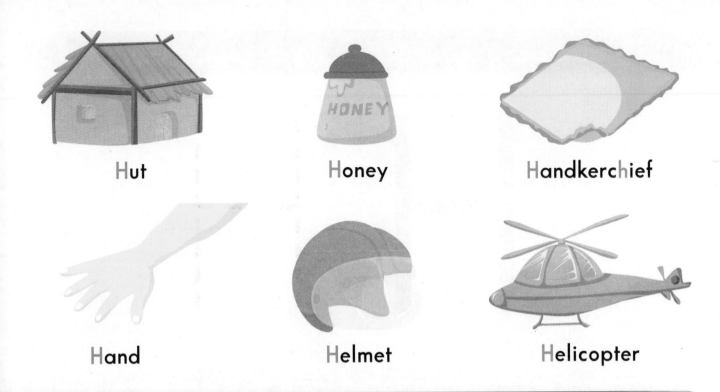

Hut

Honey

Handkerchief

Hand

Helmet

Helicopter

More words with the sound of H

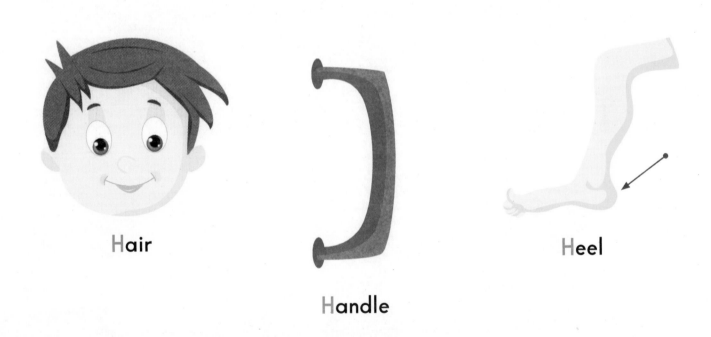

Hair

Handle

Heel

Let's read

Hand Hip Hit Hat

H H

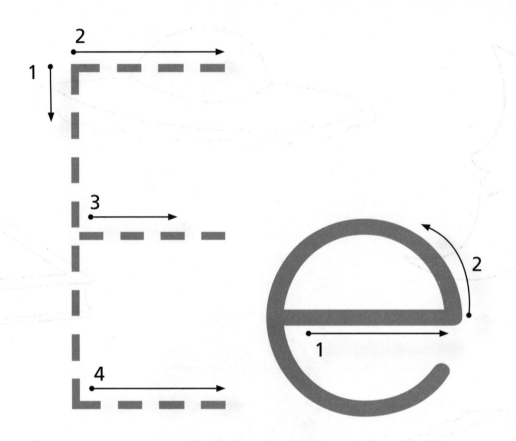

Words that begin with E

Eye

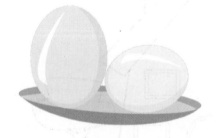

Eggs

Elephant

Engine

Ear

Eel

Elbow

Eagle

Earring

More words with the sound of E

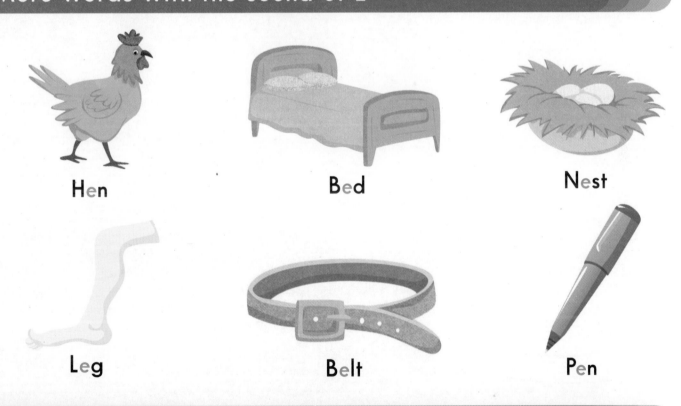

Hen

Bed

Nest

Leg

Belt

Pen

Let's read

| Pet | Net | Ten | Den | Hen |

I Learn, I Remember

In each box, colour the picture whose name begins with the letter shown.

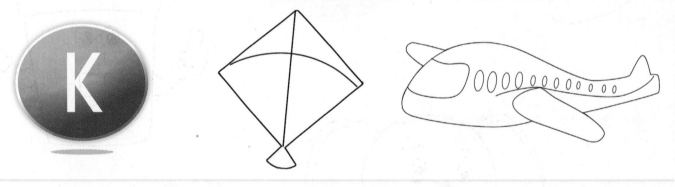

Practise writing these letters.

M   K   H   E

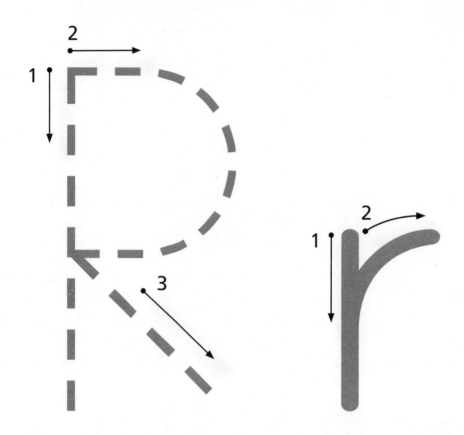

Words that begin with R

Rose

Rat

Radish

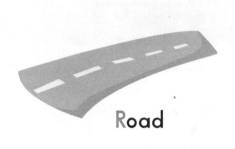

Road

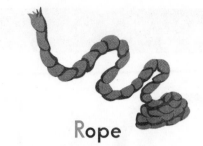

Rope

Rain

Radio

Rickshaw

Ring

More words with the sound of R

Car

Orange

Truck

Drum

Crown

Star

Let's read

Rat   Card   Star   Park   Mark   Dark

Tipi the Cat

Look at the pictures carefully to follow the story of Tipi the cat.

1. Tipi is a cat.
2. Pin is in car.
3. Tipi sat in car.
4. Pin in Tipi's pants.
5. Tipi is sad.

Words that begin with G

Grapes

Glass

Gun

Grass

Gift

Girl

Green

Goat

Guava

Mango

Bag

Fingers

Mug

Bangle

Leg

Let's read

| Tag | Dig | Gas | Gap | King | Sing |

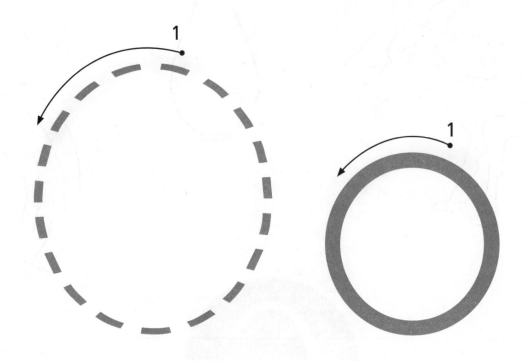

1

1

Words that begin with O

Orange

Owl

Ox

Otter

Olive

Ostrich

Onion

Oar

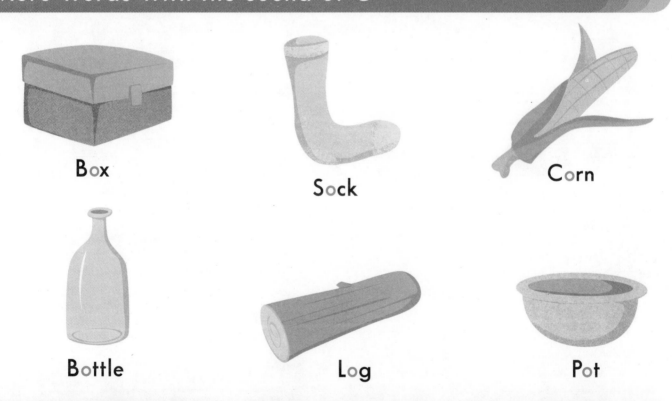

Box

Sock

Corn

Bottle

Log

Pot

Let's read

| Dog | Dot | Cot | Hot | Cop | Pond |

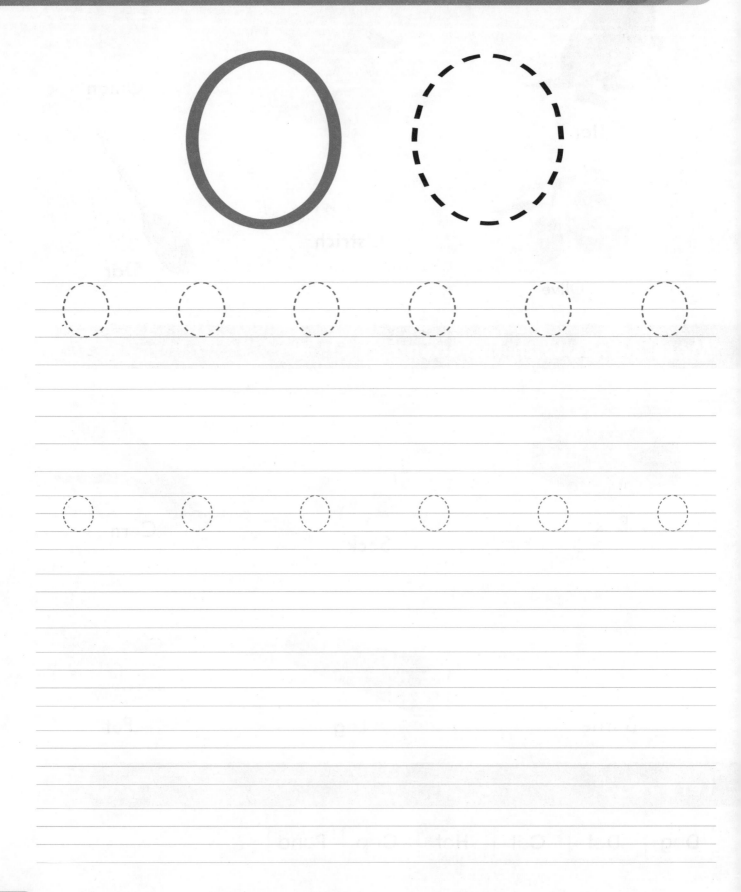

How to Make U

Words that begin with U

Uncle

Urn

Umbrella

Utensils

Unicorn

More words with the sound of U

Bus

Bulb

Tub

Turtle

Mug

Purse

Let's read

| Sun | Run | Nut | Cut | Hut | Pup |

I Learn, I Remember

In each box, colour the picture whose name begins with the letter shown.

R G O U

Match the letters to the pictures.

 K

 E

 H

 M

 O

 G

 R

How to Make L

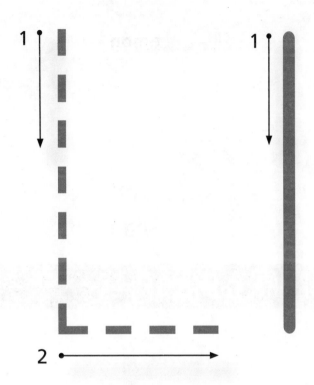

1 ↓

2 →

Words that begin with L

Lips   Lock   Lion

Lollipop

Lemon

Lizard

Leg

Lotus

Clock

Milk

Camel

Doll

Smile

Ball

Let's read

| Log | Lid | Old | Cold | Lamp |

How to Make F

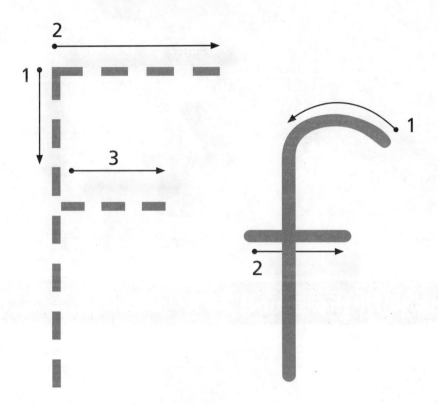

Words that begin with F

Frog

Fish

Frock

Fire   Fruits   Feather

Fan   Four   Finger

More words with the sound of F

Scarf   Sofa   Calf

Coffee   Muffler   Toffee

Let's read

Fat   Fit   Fun   Fork   Soft

Fifi is a frog.

Fifi is in a pond.

Riti is a rat.

Riti has a can.

Riti hits the can.

The can is in the pond.
Fifi helps Riti.

Fifi gets the can.

Fifi and Riti sing a song.

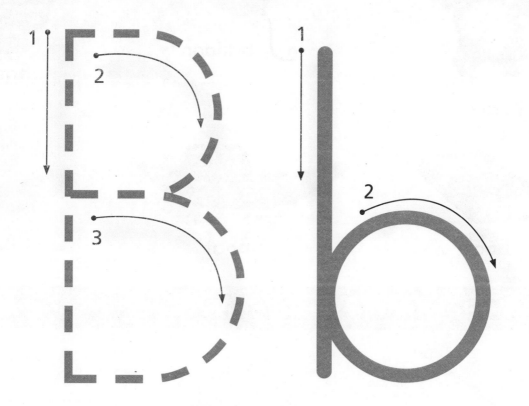

Words that begin with B

Ball

Bag

Bat

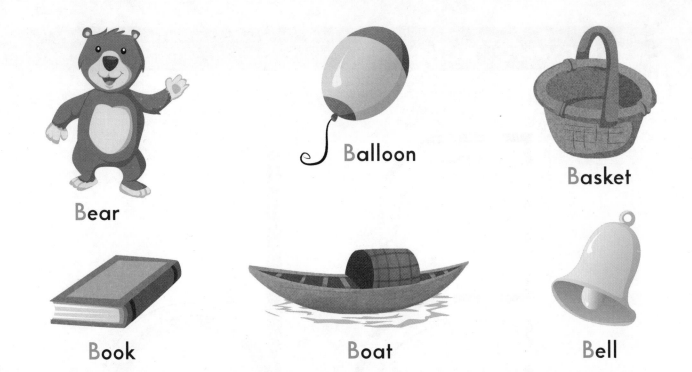

Bear

Balloon

Basket

Book

Boat

Bell

More words with the sound of B

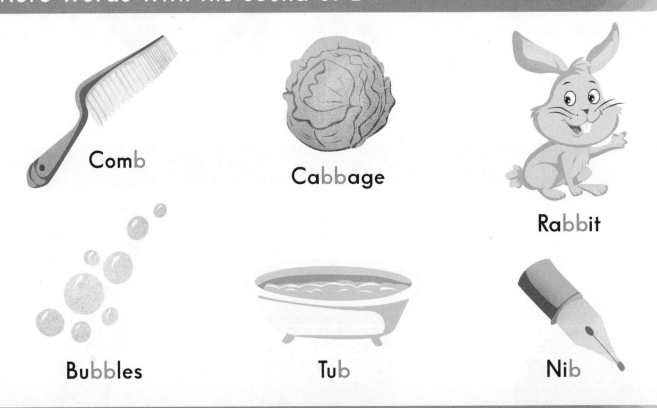

Comb

Cabbage

Rabbit

Bubbles

Tub

Nib

Let's read

| Band | Cab | Bin | Bib |

96

Rising Star: English   96

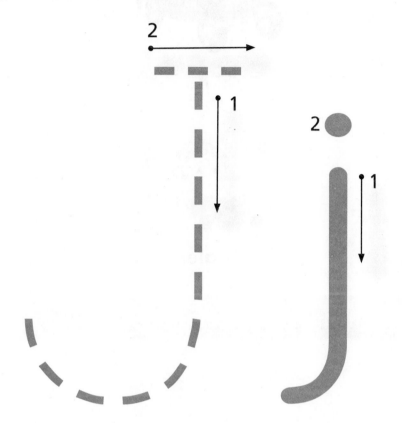

Words that begin with J

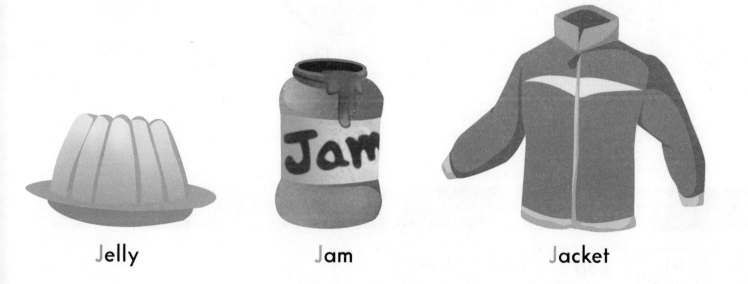

Jelly   Jam   Jacket

Joker

Jeep

Jackal

Jewel

Juggler

Jar

More words with the sound of J

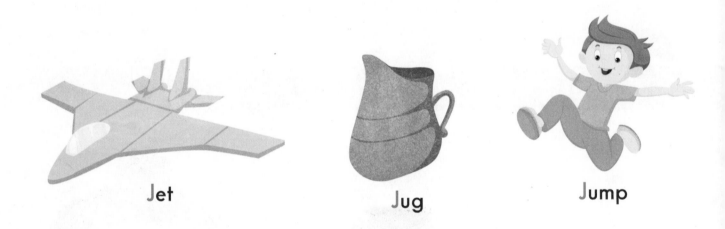

Jet

Jug

Jump

Let's read

Job | Jog | Juice | Jump

I Learn, I Remember

In each box, colour the picture whose name begins with the letter shown.

L   F   B   J

How to Make W

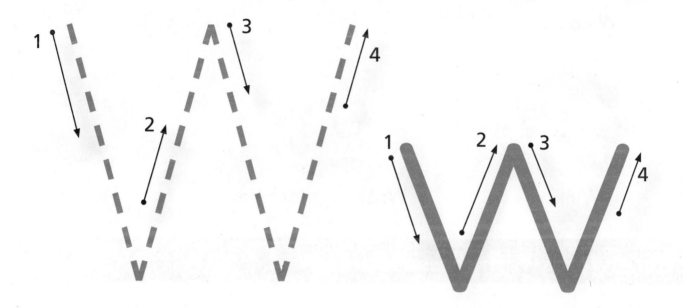

Words that begin with W

Water   Wire   Wiper

Window

Watch

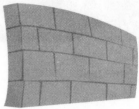

Wall

Wink

Washing machine

Wallet

More words with the sound of W

Cow

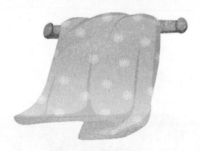

Towel

Tower

Wok

Walnut

Let's read

| Wet | Win | Wind | Wig | War | Word |

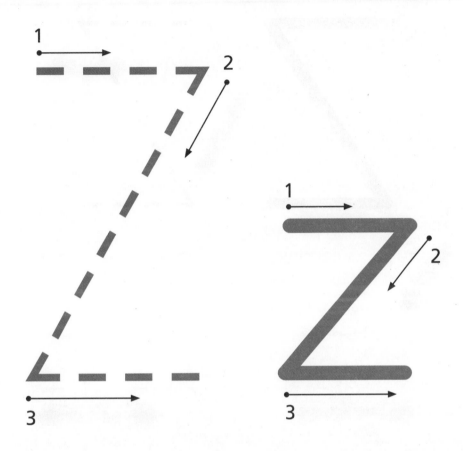

Words that begin with Z

Zero

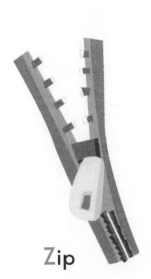

Zip

Zebra

109

Z Z

Picture Reading

1. What is the boy doing?
2. What is the girl doing?
3. How many ants do you see?
4. Which insect do you see on the leaf below?

How to Make Y

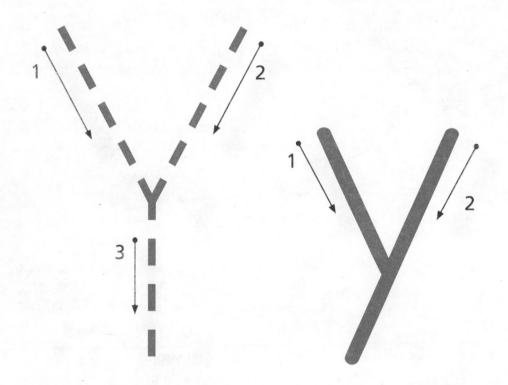

Words that begin with Y

Yak　　　Yoyo　　　Yacht　　　Yam

How to Make X

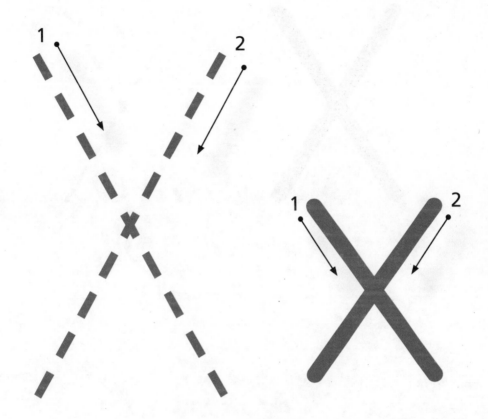

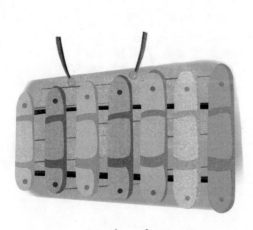

Xylophone

X-ray

More words with the sound of Z

Puzzle

Prize

Razor

Blazer

More words with the sound of Y

Boy

Toy

Yoga

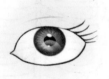

Eye

More words with the sound of X

Ox

Box

Fox

Mixer

Taxi

Six

Exercise

Jim has a bat. Mini has a car.

Jim and Mini sit in the car and go to the park.

Ben has a ball.
Jim Mini and Ben play.

Jim hits ball with bat.
Mini gets the ball.

Draw a line to show these children the way to the things they want.

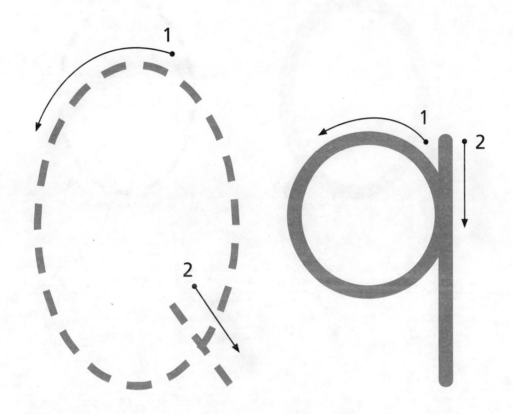

Words that begin with Q

Queen

Quilt

Quill

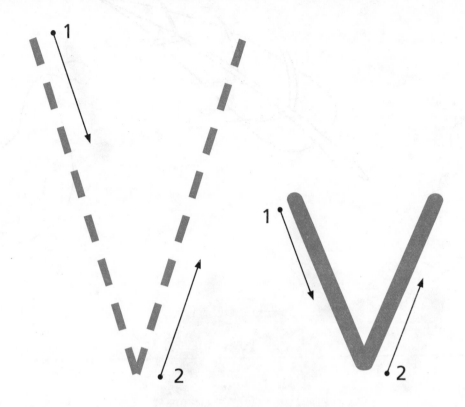

Words that begin with V

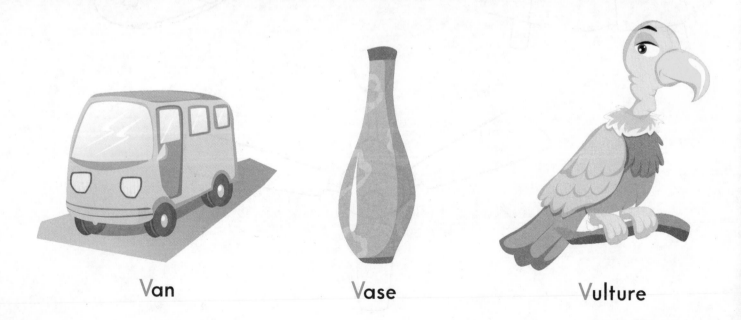

Van

Vase

Vulture

More words with the sound of Q

Quail   Squirrel   Square

More words with the sound of V

Five

Dove

Gloves

Cave

I Learn, I Remember

In each box, colour the picture whose name begins with the letter shown.

  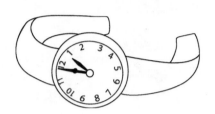

  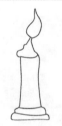

 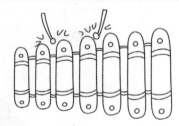 

Practise writing these letters.

W   Z   Y   X   Q   V

F

 J

 W

 Z

 Y

 X

 Q

 V

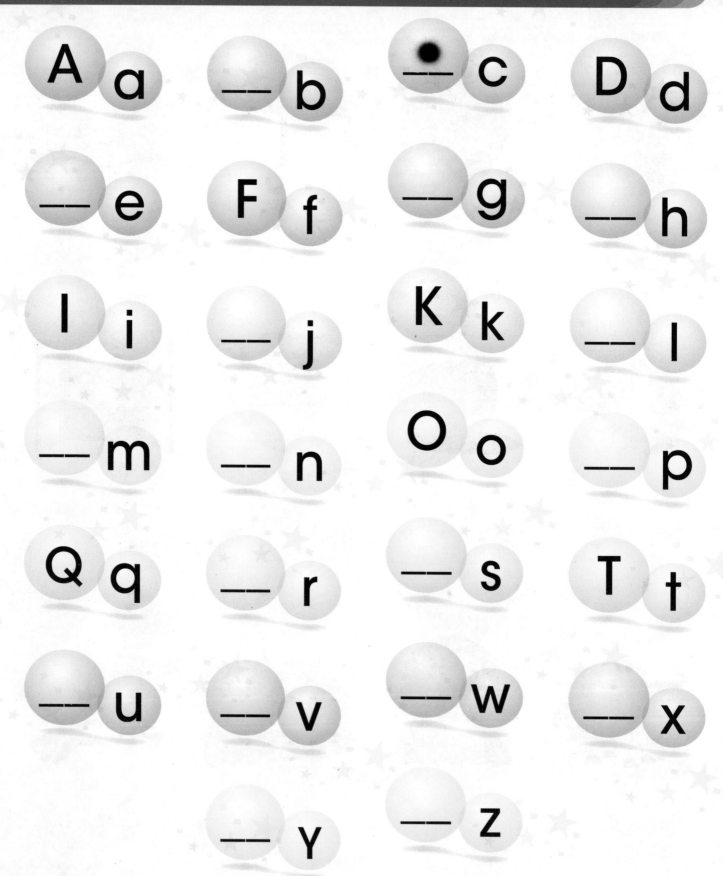

A a
__ b
__ c
D d
__ e
F f
__ g
__ h
I i
__ j
K k
__ l
__ m
__ n
O o
__ p
Q q
__ r
__ s
T t
__ u
__ v
__ w
__ x
__ y
__ z

A

B

C

D

E

F

G

H

c

e

g

a

b

h

d

f

I

J

K

L

M

N

O

P

Q

l

m

p

i

o

q

j

k

n

R	u
S	x
T	r
U	y
V	z
W	t
X	s
Y	w
Z	v

Aa   Bb   Cc   Dd   Ee   Ff

Gg   Hh   Ii   Jj   Kk   Ll

Mm   Nn   Oo   Pp   Qq   Rr

Ss   Tt   Uu   Vv   Ww   Xx

Yy   Zz

Write A to Z in sequence.

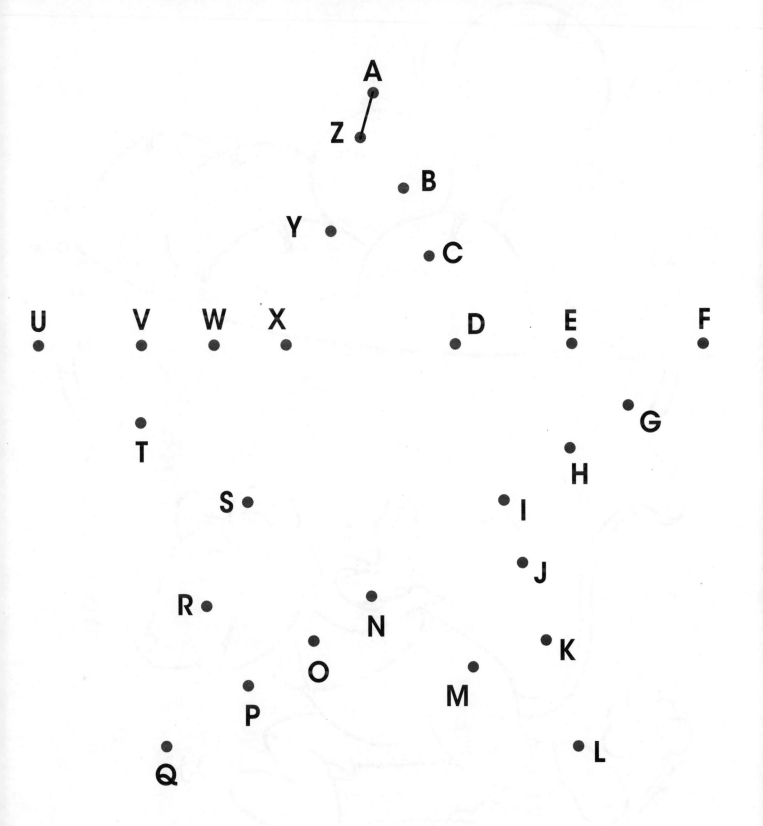

NOTES